2/03

Festive Foods for the Holidays™

A Kwanzaa Holiday
COOKBOOK

Emily Raabe

The Rosen Publishing Group's
PowerKids Press™
New York

The recipes in this cookbook
are intended for a child to make together with an adult.

Many thanks to Ruth Rosen and her test kitchen

For Rachel, my favorite chef

Published in 2002 by The Rosen Publishing Group, Inc.
29 East 21st Street, New York, NY 10010

Copyright © 2002 by The Rosen Publishing Group, Inc.

First Edition

Book Design: Maria E. Melendez
Layout Design: Kim Sonsky
Project Editor: Frances E. Ruffin

Photo Credits: Cover and title page, family celebrating Kwanzaa, p. 21 © Index Stock; Cover and title page, (mangos, papaya, lemons, potatoes, coconut, corn, peanuts, black-eyed peas, bananas) © Digital Stock; p. 4 (Portrait of Dr. Maulana Karenga) © Hakim Mutlaq; p. 8, 13, 17 © SuperStock; pp. 4, 8, 13, 17, 21 fruit pot designs created by Maria E. Melendez; All recipe photos by Arlan Dean.

Raabe, Emily.
 A Kwanzaa holiday cookbook / Emily Raabe.— 1st ed.
  p. cm. — (Festive foods for the holidays)
 Includes bibliographical references and index.
  ISBN 0-8239-5629-6 (lib. binding)
 1. Kwanzaa—Juvenile literature. 2. African American cookery—Juvenile literature. 3. Cookery, African—Juvenile literature. [1. Kwanzaa. 2. African American cookery.] I. Title. II. Series.
 GT4403 .R33 2002

Manufactured in the United States of America

Contents

What Is Kwanzaa?

Like Christmas and Hanukkah, Kwanzaa is **celebrated** in December. Unlike Christmas or Hanukkah, Kwanzaa is not a religious holiday. Kwanzaa is a time for African Americans to celebrate their roots in Africa, as well as their lives as Americans. In the 1960s, a man in California named Dr. Maulana Karenga decided that African Americans needed a time to get together to celebrate their **culture**. In December 1966, Dr. Karenga announced a new holiday. He called this holiday Kwanzaa. In **Swahili**, kwanza means "first." This holiday lasts seven days, from December 26 to January 1.

Dr. Karenga is shown at the left. In Africa, people celebrate "matunda ya kwanza," or "first fruits."

Kwanzaa Means First

Swahili is a common language spoken in Africa. To remind African Americans of their African **heritage**, people celebrating Kwanzaa use many Swahili words. For example, Dr. Karenga took the Swahili word kwanza, which means "first," and added an extra *a* at the end of the word. Kwanzaa spelled with two *a*'s is a new word. This new word mixes together African and American words. "Benne" is the Swahili name for sesame seeds. Cake, of course, is a word used in America. If you make Benne cakes, you will be mixing words from Africa and America in your own kitchen! These "cakes" are more like cookies.

6

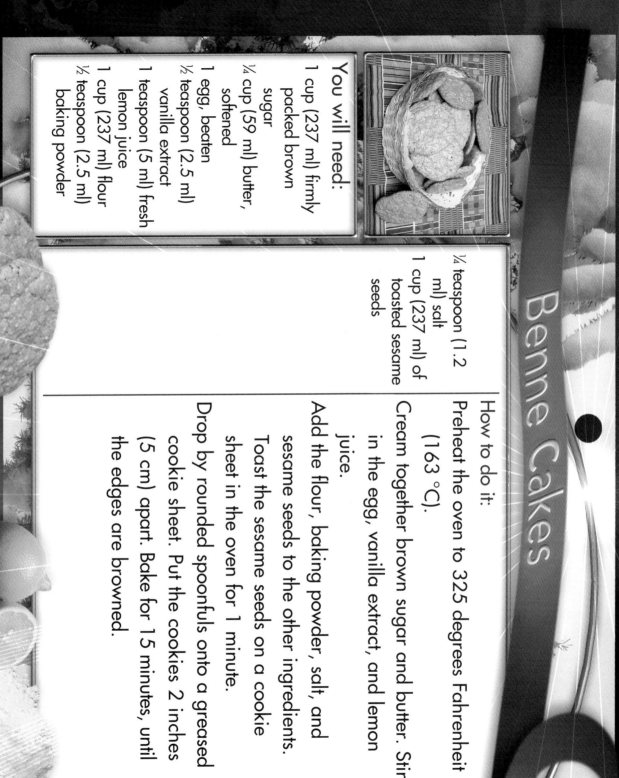

You will need:

- 1 cup (237 ml) firmly packed brown sugar
- ¼ cup (59 ml) butter, softened
- 1 egg, beaten
- ½ teaspoon (2.5 ml) vanilla extract
- 1 teaspoon (5 ml) fresh lemon juice
- 1 cup (237 ml) flour
- ½ teaspoon (2.5 ml) baking powder
- ¼ teaspoon (1.2 ml) salt
- 1 cup (237 ml) of toasted sesame seeds

How to do it:

Preheat the oven to 325 degrees Fahrenheit (163 °C).

Cream together brown sugar and butter. Stir in the egg, vanilla extract, and lemon juice.

Add the flour, baking powder, salt, and sesame seeds to the other ingredients.

Toast the sesame seeds on a cookie sheet in the oven for 1 minute.

Drop by rounded spoonfuls onto a greased cookie sheet. Put the cookies 2 inches (5 cm) apart. Bake for 15 minutes, until the edges are browned.

The Seven Principles of Kwanzaa

There are seven **principles**, or beliefs, that are practiced during Kwanzaa. These beliefs are called the Nguzo Saba (in-GOO-zoh SAH-bah). They are beliefs are called the Umoja (oo-MOW-ja), or **unity**; Kujichagulia (koo-jee-cha-GOO-lee-ah), being in charge of your life; Ujima (oo-jEE-mah), working together and caring for others; Ujamaa (oo-jAH-mah), supporting others' work; Nia (NEE-ah), purpose; Kuumba (koo-OOM-bah), **creativity**; and Imani (ee-MAH-nee), faith. One principle is celebrated on each day of Kwanzaa. People greet each other by saying, "Ha bari gani?" or "What is the news?" They answer each other with the principle for the day. On the first day of Kwanzaa, they would say, "Umoja," or "Unity."

During Kwanzaa, African Americans may make skits, sing songs, or tell stories about each day's Nguzo Saba.

The Seven Symbols of Kwanzaa

Just as there are seven beliefs to Kwanzaa, there are also seven **symbols** that people use to celebrate Kwanzaa. These symbols also have Swahili names. They are the *Mkeka* (muh-KAY-kah), a straw mat; the *Karamu* (kah-RAH-moo), the feast; the *Kikombe Cha Umoja* (kee-COMB-bay CHAH oo-MOW-jah), the unity cup; the *Kinara* (kee-NAR-ah), the candleholder, and seven candles, which are called *Mishumaa Saba* (mee-SHOO-mah SA-bah); the *Muhindi* (moo-HEEN-dee), or ears of corn—one for each child; and the *Zawadi* (zah-WAH-dee), Kwanzaa gifts. Each symbol comes from African or African American culture. You can make a delicious treat at Kwanzaa using corn. Serve this cornbread hot from the oven to your Kwanzaa guests.

10

Kwanzaa Cornbread

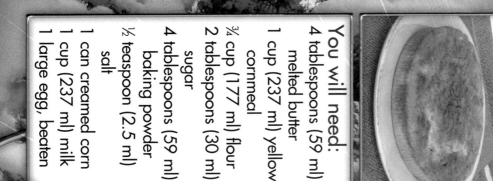

You will need:

- 4 tablespoons (59 ml) melted butter
- 1 cup (237 ml) yellow cornmeal
- ¾ cup (177 ml) flour
- 2 tablespoons (30 ml) sugar
- 4 tablespoons (59 ml) baking powder
- ½ teaspoon (2.5 ml) salt
- 1 can creamed corn
- 1 cup (237 ml) milk
- 1 large egg, beaten

How to do it:

Preheat the oven to 450 degrees Fahrenheit (232 °C).

Pour 2 tablespoons (30 ml) of the melted butter into the cake pan and wait until it melts. Be careful—the cake pan will become very hot! Put the pan aside.

Mix cornmeal, flour, sugar, baking powder, and salt in a medium bowl.

Make a well in the center of the dry ingredients and pour in the beaten egg, the remaining butter, 14 ounces (41 cl) creamed-style corn, and the milk. Stir until the batter is smooth and pour the batter into the hot pan.

Bake for 30–35 minutes until a toothpick stuck in the cornbread comes out clean. Let the cornbread stand for 20 minutes before you serve it.

The Kwanzaa Table

Each symbol on the Kwanzaa table has a meaning in the celebration. The Mkeka, or woven mat, can be made of grass, straw, cotton, or sometimes paper. All of the other Kwanzaa symbols are placed on the Mkeka. The fruit on the Kwanzaa table is a symbol of good things and a good harvest. The cup of unity is used in the Kwanzaa ceremony. One of each of the seven Kwanzaa candles is lit each night. The ears of corn on the Kwanzaa table **represent** the children in the family that is celebrating this holiday.

The first three candles in the Kinara are red, symbolizing hard work and a rich life. The center candle, which is lit on the first night of Kwanzaa, is black. This candle represents the African and African American people. The last three candles are green, representing hope for the future.

12

Kwanzaa Foods

As with holidays all over the world, Kwanzaa means a lot of good food! Food for Kwanzaa is usually a mix of African foods, such as yams (sweet potatoes), peanuts, and okra, and African American foods. African Americans who live in the southern United States might eat black-eyed peas and rice, fried chicken, cornbread, sweet potato pie, and coconut cake during their Kwanzaa celebrations. African Americans whose relatives are from the Caribbean might eat red beans and rice with chicken for Kwanzaa. You can make these sweet potato fritters for your Kwanzaa meal. Whether you call them yams or sweet potatoes, they are definitely delicious!

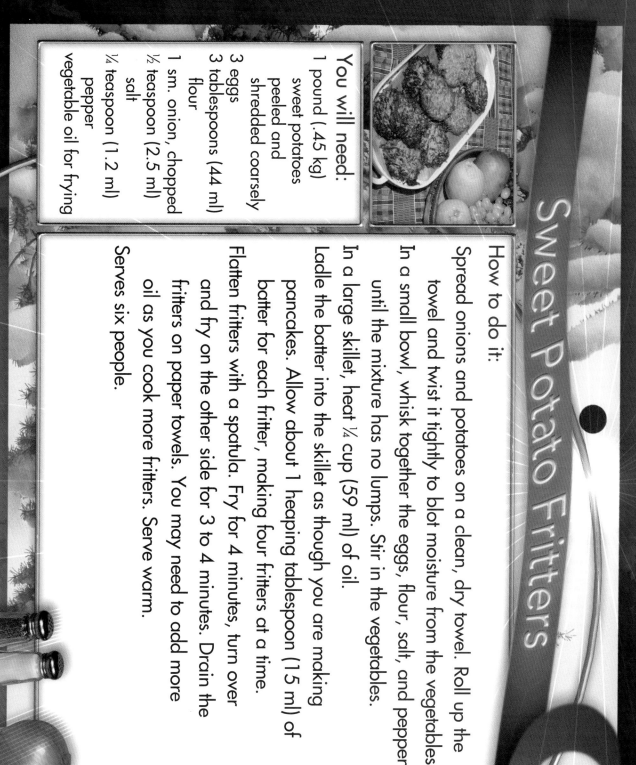

You will need:

- 1 pound (.45 kg) sweet potatoes peeled and shredded coarsely
- 3 eggs
- 3 tablespoons (44 ml) flour
- 1 sm. onion, chopped
- ½ teaspoon (2.5 ml) salt
- ¼ teaspoon (1.2 ml) pepper
- vegetable oil for frying

How to do it:

Spread onions and potatoes on a clean, dry towel. Roll up the towel and twist it tightly to blot moisture from the vegetables.

In a small bowl, whisk together the eggs, flour, salt, and pepper until the mixture has no lumps. Stir in the vegetables.

In a large skillet, heat ¼ cup (59 ml) of oil.

Ladle the batter into the skillet as though you are making pancakes. Allow about 1 heaping tablespoon (15 ml) of batter for each fritter, making four fritters at a time.

Flatten fritters with a spatula. Fry for 4 minutes, turn over and fry on the other side for 3 to 4 minutes. Drain the fritters on paper towels. You may need to add more oil as you cook more fritters. Serve warm.

Serves six people.

Celebrating Kwanzaa

Many African Americans decorate their homes with red, black, and green streamers, balloons, or cloths for Kwanzaa. They may wear African clothing during Kwanzaa, and they may hang photographs or pictures of African American leaders and heroes around the house. Some adults **fast** from sunup to sundown during Kwanzaa, eating only the evening meal. At night, family and friends gather and light a candle on the *Kinara*. They might talk about or tell a story about the *Nguzo Saba* for that day. People share a sip of water from the cup of unity in honor of dead relatives. Then everyone sits down to share a meal and celebrate Kwanzaa.

During Kwanzaa, African American women might wear a style of gown called a buba and cover their hair with an African wrap known as a gela. Men and women wear a traditional African robe called a dashiki.

16

Karamu

The last night of Kwanzaa is celebrated with a feast called the *Karamu*. The *Karamu* is a joyful night of song, dance, prayer, and feasting with family and friends. It is the night that people give one another Kwanzaa gifts, or *Zawadi*. These gifts are often homemade, and they reflect the principles of the holiday that are listed in the *Nguzo Saba*. As with the other nights of Kwanzaa, the foods on the table are based on recipes from Africa and from all over America. Chicken, either fried or prepared with coconut, as in this recipe, is a popular Kwanzaa dish. These coconut chicken chews make an easy and delicious Kwanzaa food that reflects both African and African American cooking.

18

You will need:

- 1 cup (237 ml) of sweetened, flaked coconut
- 1 cup (237 ml) flour
- ½ teaspoon (2.5 ml) salt
- ¼ teaspoon (1.2 ml) pepper
- 1½ pounds (.68 kg) boneless, skinless chicken breasts
- ⅓ cup (78 ml) butter, melted

How to do it:

Preheat the oven to 400 degrees Fahrenheit (204 °C).

Combine coconut, flour, salt, and pepper in a paper bag.

Cut the chicken breasts into 1-inch (2.5-cm) strips.

Dip a chicken strip into the beaten egg, then put it into the bag of spices and shake it, holding the bag closed (you also can use a plastic Zip-lock bag for this). When the chicken is coated with the coconut mixture, place it in a shallow baking pan. Repeat this step until all of the chicken is in the baking pan.

Drizzle ⅓ cup (78 ml) melted butter over the chicken. Bake for 25 minutes, turning once.

Serve chicken chews with a bowl of apricot preserves for a dipping sauce. This recipe makes about 2 dozen coconut chicken chews.

The Ceremony of Karamu

Different families celebrate the *Karamu*, or the feast night of Kwanzaa, in different ways. Usually there is a speech at the beginning of the night. The person who gives the speech is an elder, an older member of the group. On this night, all seven candles are lit while people recite each of the seven *Nguzo Saba*. The unity cup is filled and passed around so that everyone may take a sip from it. A little bit of water is spilled out to honor **ancestors**. Then, of course, there is a long and joyful feast!

During Karamu someone will stand up and talk about what one of the Nguzo Saba means to him or her. Some people also may sing, put on skits, or tell stories about the Nguzo Saba.

20

Kwanzaa All Year Long

At the end of the *Karamu*, there is a farewell speech, and then everyone in the room shouts *"Harambee* (ha-RAHM-bee)" seven times. *Harambee* is Swahili for "Let's pull together!" Shouting "*Harambee*" reminds people that Kwanzaa is a celebration of working together and making communities better, stronger, and healthier.

Although Kwanzaa comes only once a year, you can practice Kwanzaa all year long. Just remember the seven *Nguzo Saba* and you can help to make your own community a better place. You also can cook your new Kwanzaa recipes for your friends and family. No matter what time of year it is, they will thank you!

Glossary

ancestors (AN-ses-turz) Relatives who lived a long time ago.

celebrated (SEH-luh-brayt-ed) Having observed a special time or day with festive activities.

creativity (kree-ay-TIH-vuh-tee) The ability to have good, new ideas.

culture (KUL-cher) The beliefs, customs, art, and religions of a group of people.

fast (FAST-ing) To go without food.

heritage (HAYR-ih-tij) The cultural traditions that are handed down from parent to child.

principles (PRIN-sih-pulz) Beliefs or ways of behaving.

represent (reh-prih-ZENT) To stand for something.

Swahili (swah-HEE-lee) A language that is spoken in many countries of Africa.

symbols (SIM-bulz) Objects or designs that stand for something important.

unity (YOO-nih-tee) Togetherness.

23

Index

A
Africa, 5, 6, 18
African American(s), 5, 6, 10, 14, 16

B
Benne cakes, 6

C
coconut chicken chews, 18

F
fast, 16

I
Imani, 9

K
Karamu, 10, 18, 20, 22
Karenga, Dr. Maulana, 5, 6
Kikombe Cha Umoja, 10
Kinara, 10, 16
Kujichagulia, 9
Kuumba, 9

M
Mishumaa Saba, 10
Mkeka, 10, 12
Muhindi, 10

N
Nguzo Saba, 9, 16, 18, 20, 22
Nia, 9

S
Swahili, 5, 6, 10, 22
sweet potato fritters, 14

U
Ujamaa, 9
Ujima, 9
Umoja, 9

Z
Zawadi, 10, 18

Web Sites

To learn more about Kwanzaa, check out these Web sites:
www.afroam.org/children/fun/kwanzaa/kwanzaa.html
www.officialkwanzaawebsite.org

24